First Picture
Encyclopedia
of
Animals

by Belinda Gallagher

illustrated by Lucy Semple

ARCTURUS

This edition published in 2024 by Arcturus Publishing Limited
26/27 Bickels Yard, 151–153 Bermondsey Street,
London SE1 3HA

Author: Belinda Gallagher
Illustrator: Lucy Semple
Editor: Violet Peto
Designer: Simon Oliver
Consultant: Anne Rooney
Managing editor: Joe Harris
Design manager: Rosie Bellwood-Moyler

ISBN: 978-1-3988-4471-1
CH011580NT
Supplier 29, Date 0724, Print run 00006669

Printed in China

Contents

Animal Life

From elephants to ants, animals are found almost everywhere on earth. Today we know about more than 1.5 million types, or species, of animals. And more will be discovered in the future! Each animal is perfectly suited to survive where it lives.

What Is an Animal?

- It's a living thing that breathes air.

- It has a body that can move.

- It finds food, which gives it energy.

- It uses its senses to find out about the world.

- An animal reproduces to have young.

Sloth

Animal Homes

The place where an animal lives is called its habitat. Oceans, forests, deserts, and grasslands are all types of habitats. This sloth and her baby live high up in rain forest trees.

Hummingbird

Animal Groups

There are six main animal groups—mammals, birds, reptiles, amphibians, fish, and invertebrates. This hummingbird belongs to the bird group.

Dragonfly

Animal Bodies

Many animals have a hard skeleton with a backbone inside their bodies—they are vertebrates. Animals without a backbone, like this dragonfly, are invertebrates.

All About Mammals

Our planet is home to thousands of kinds of mammals. They live in almost every habitat on land and in water. All mammals are warm-blooded, which means they can keep their body temperature at a constant level. Most are covered in fur or hair, and baby mammals feed on milk produced by their mothers.

Arctic fox

Because mammals are warm-blooded, they can live in some of the planet's coldest places. The Arctic fox has very thick fur to keep out the cold. This stops it from losing too much body heat.

ZEBRA

I'm this big:

This is where I live: grasslands and plains of Africa

I eat: grasses, leaves, twigs, bark

Bonus fact: My skin is black, but my fur is striped.

Zebra

The biggest group of mammals is the rodent family. The red squirrel belongs to this group. It has excellent senses and gnawing teeth that never stop growing.

Caring for Young

Mammal mothers take good care of their young. This newborn zebra foal can already stand to keep close to its mother and feed on her milk.

Red squirrel

Cats

Sharp claws and teeth, and super senses make cats superb hunters. Their flexible bodies can bend and twist, and strong muscles help them run and leap. Cats range in size from the pets we have at home to the biggest of all—the tiger. All cats are covered in fur and have padded paws to help them creep up on prey.

Lion

These huge African cats live in family groups called prides. Males are much bigger than females and have a big ruff of fur called a mane. Cubs are very playful, and this helps them learn hunting skills.

Beautiful markings on their coat help jaguars blend in with their rain forest home. These big cats are excellent swimmers. They live in swampy jungle habitats where they hunt deer—and even caimans, a type of crocodile!

Jaguar

Hunting by Stealth

Tigers use camouflage to help them hunt. The black stripes on their orange fur help to hide them in long grass. They crouch down low and silently creep up on prey before pouncing with powerful paws. Tigers usually have just one big meal a week. Many of their hunts are unsuccessful.

Tiger

TIGER

I'm this big:

This is where I live: thick forests and plains of southern and eastern Asia

I eat: deer, wild boar, birds, monkeys, fish

Bonus fact: India has more wild tigers than any other country—about 3,000.

Dogs

This group of mammals is very well-known to us—it includes the pet dogs we have at home. In the wild, dogs include wolves, foxes, coyotes, jackals, and dingos. There are about 34 different species, and together they are known as canines. Dogs have long legs for chasing prey and incredible senses of smell and hearing.

Gray wolf

Living as a Pack

With long muzzles, sharp teeth, and powerful bodies, gray wolves (sometimes called grey wolves) are skilled hunters. They live in northern parts of the world in family groups called packs. The biggest members of the dog family, gray wolves are clever animals. They communicate by howling, growling, and yelping, and by using body language.

Built for running long distances, African wild dogs can hunt prey much bigger than they are. By working as a team, they cover long distances without stopping to rest.

African wild dog

The fennec fox is the smallest member of the dog family. This desert fox has big bat-like ears that help it keep cool by losing body heat. By day, it sleeps underground. In the evening, it creeps out to hunt insects and lizards to eat.

Fennec fox

GRAY WOLF

I'm this big:

This is where I live: forest, woodland, and tundra of northern Europe, America, and Asia

I eat: deer, caribou, bison, birds, rabbits, hares

Bonus fact: If I am scared, I flatten my ears, tuck my tail under, and lower my body.

Bears

These mammals have stocky bodies, large paws, and sharp claws. There are eight species of bears, and they live in many different habitats, from the icy Arctic to thick forests. Most bears are omnivores—they eat plants as well as other animals. They use their powerful sense of smell to find food.

Female polar bears dig a snow den in which to have their cubs. This keeps them warm and safe until spring. The cubs have the summer to grow big enough to survive in their freezing Arctic home. Polar bears are meat-eaters.

Polar bear

BROWN BEAR

I'm this big:

This is where I live: forests, woodlands, and mountains of northern America, Europe, and Asia

I eat: shoots, fruit, berries, nuts, insects, and other animals such as small mammals and fish

Bonus fact: North American brown bears are also known as grizzlies.

Fishing for Salmon

Brown bears are huge—they have big appetites, too. In parts of North America, they have learned to hunt salmon as they leap upstream. These bears are often the biggest because the salmon provide lots of goodness. Brown bears eat as much as they can before winter to pile on fat. Then they find a warm place to sleep until the spring.

Unlike other bears, the giant panda feeds almost entirely on just one plant—bamboo. To get enough goodness from their diet, pandas eat for up to 12 hours a day!

Brown bear

Giant panda

Monkeys and Apes

Clever animals, monkeys and apes live mainly in tropical forests. Monkeys are smaller than apes and have tails. They move through the trees by running along branches, using their strong tails to grip. Apes use their arms to swing through the forest and spend more time on the ground than monkeys. There are just six kinds of apes, and most have learned how to use simple tools, such as sticks.

Japanese macaques

In parts of Japan, macaques have learned a clever way to keep warm when temperatures drop. They sit in the steamy waters of natural hot springs! Japanese macaques live farther north than any other type of monkey. They are also known as snow monkeys.

Red howler monkey

The whooping calls of red howler monkeys can be heard from up to 5 km (3 miles) away. Their howls tell other monkeys to look out for danger—or to keep away—this is our patch!

Gentle Giants

In the cloud forests of Africa live the biggest of all apes—mountain gorillas. They have long, shaggy fur to keep them warm and live in family groups led by a huge male called a silverback. All members of the group help care for the young. Every night, gorillas make nests from leaves and plants in which to sleep.

Mountain gorillas

MOUNTAIN GORILLA

I'm this big:

This is where I live: high up in the thick mountain forests of Africa

I eat: shoots, leaves, stems, fruit, bark, and sometimes ants

Bonus fact: If threatened, a silverback may charge and beat his chest with his hands.

Rabbits and Hares

Fast, furry, and with super senses, rabbits and hares live almost everywhere on land. They are an important food source for other animals, and females have lots of babies throughout the year. Rabbits are smaller than hares, and their young are born with eyes closed and no fur. Baby hares are born covered in fur and with eyes open.

Perfect Camouflage

Arctic hares are perfectly suited to their icy habitat. Thick, white fur keeps them warm and blends in with their surroundings. To keep them from losing body heat, they have smaller ears than other hares. In spring, the white fur is replaced by a new brown coat. This provides camouflage as the Arctic ice melts.

Arctic hare

In the spring, hares can be seen "boxing." The male chases the female, but if she isn't interested in him, she will stop and box with him! Males also box with each other to compete for females. Baby hares are called leverets.

European hares

Always on the lookout for danger, rabbits sit upright, noses twitching, listening. If scared, they will bolt for cover. Baby rabbits are called kittens.

Baby rabbits (kittens)

ARCTIC HARE

I'm this big:

This is where I live: Arctic tundra of Canada and Greenland

I eat: mostly woody plants, as well as lichen, moss, grasses

Bonus fact: In winter, Arctic hares sometimes flock together in their hundreds.

Elephants

The biggest animals to live on land, elephants are true giants. They have bulky bodies, strong legs, big ears, and a long trunk. There are three species of elephant: the African bush, the African forest, and the Asian elephant.

African bush elephant

African bush elephants are the biggest. They live in herds on the plains and grasslands. Bush elephants also have bigger ears and longer tusks than other species.

The smaller African forest elephant lives in thick rain forests. It also has tusks that point downward, allowing it to move more freely through trees and thick undergrowth.

African forest elephant

We Are Family

All elephants live in family groups called herds. The herd is led by an older female called a matriarch. These gentle creatures are very intelligent. They work together to find food and water, and to take care of each other. Baby elephants are protected by all members of the herd. Asian elephants are smaller than African. They mainly live in India.

Asian elephants

AFRICAN FOREST ELEPHANT

I'm this big:

This is where I live: tropical forests in Central and West Africa

I eat: leaves, grasses, fruit, seeds, tree bark

Bonus fact: I flap my ears to help keep me cool in hot weather!

Sloths

Slow-moving sloths live in the canopy of the rain forest. They hang from the branches with long, curved claws, eating and sleeping. Sloth fur is thick and grows in a direction that allows rain to drip off, so the sloth stays dry. Shaggy sloth fur is also home to tiny plants and insects!

Anteaters are sloths' closest living relatives, even though they are very different animals. Also from South America, anteaters have long, shaggy fur, poor eyesight, but a powerful sense of smell. They use their long, strong claws to rip open ants' nests.

Giant anteater

BROWN-THROATED THREE-TOED SLOTH

I'm this big:

This is where I live: the canopy of thick tropical rain forests of South and Central America

I eat: mainly leaves

Bonus fact: There are three-toed and two-toed sloth species.

Hanging Around

Just because they move slowly doesn't mean that sloths are lazy. Being slow-moving is a good way to survive. Sloths use very little energy, and this is helpful because they are fussy eaters and get very little goodness from the leaves they eat. Baby sloths cling to their mothers and learn which leaves to eat by watching them.

The pygmy three-toed sloth is a good swimmer. It can drop into the waters around its island mangrove home to look for a mate or find new trees to live in. It can swim much faster than it moves on land.

Brown-throated sloth

Pygmy three-toed sloth

Marsupials

Unlike most mammals, marsupials give birth to their young at a very early stage. The tiny, helpless baby is fed on its mother's milk, within a pouch. Marsupials include animals such as kangaroos, koalas, possums, and sugar gliders. Marsupials move in different ways, such as running, hopping, climbing, or gliding!

Red kangaroo

Kangaroo Power

The biggest marsupial is the red kangaroo of Australia. It can bound along at top speed on long, powerful legs. A baby is called a joey, and it stays in its mother's pouch for the first few months of life. Kangaroos live in small groups called mobs. Sometimes they gather in much larger numbers around a watering hole.

Koala

Koalas live in Australia among eucalyptus trees. Leaves from this tree are the only food that koalas will eat. This leafy diet also provides liquid, so koalas have very little need to drink water.

These tree-loving marsupials live in the cool forests of Australia. They are nocturnal and glide from tree to tree by spreading the flaps of skin between their legs. Big eyes help them see in the dark.

Sugar glider

RED KANGAROO

I'm this big:

This is where I live: grassland, desert, scrubland of Australia

I eat: grasses, flowering plants, shrubs

Bonus fact: When first born, a kangaroo joey is the size of a jelly bean.

Bats

Like all mammals, bats are warm-blooded with furry bodies. But these strange-looking animals have one key difference. They can fly! Bat wings are formed from extra-long finger bones, with a covering of thin skin. At night, bats come out to feed, hunting insects and drinking nectar—or feasting on blood.

Bats are nocturnal, and during the day they rest in caves, old buildings, or trees. This is called roosting. They hang upside down, using their claws to grip, and close their wings.

Fruit bat roosting (spotted-winged fruit bat)

Vampire bat

The vampire bat feeds entirely on blood. With razor-sharp teeth, it preys on sleeping cattle or horses.

Hunting by Echoes

Bats have a clever way of hunting insects and finding their way around, called echolocation. They make very high-pitched squeaks, which travel out as sound waves. When the waves hit something, an echo bounces back to the bat. Immediately, the bat can find exactly where the insect is and swoop in and snap it up.

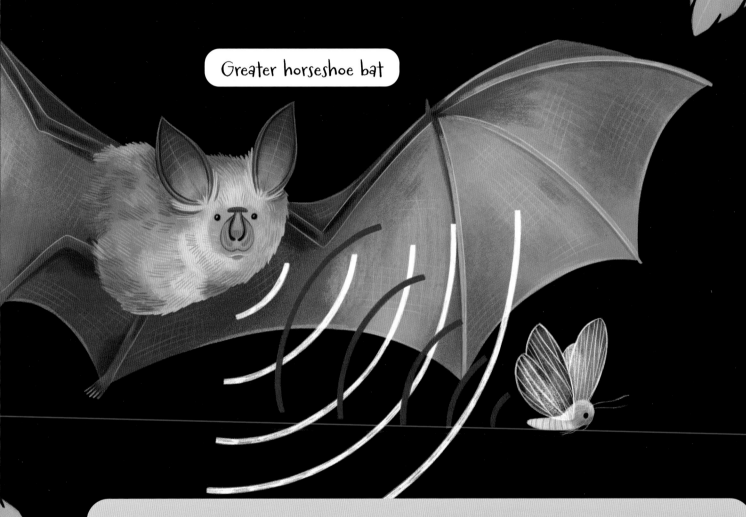

Greater horseshoe bat

GREATER HORSESHOE BAT

I'm this big:

This is where I live: meadows, woodland, and hedgerows across Europe, North Africa, and Asia

I eat: moths, beetles, flies, spiders

Bonus fact: I get my name from my fleshy, horseshoe-shaped nose.

Seals

Seals, sea lions, and walruses make up the mammal group called pinnipeds. They have smooth, sleek bodies and strong flippers for swimming. Underwater, they are speedy and graceful, but on land they haul their hefty bodies along. Sea lions have small external ears, while most seals do not. Walruses grow long tusks.

Galápagos sea lion with pup

Like most other pinnipeds, the Galápagos sea lion lives in groups. Its main home is the Galápagos Islands in the Pacific Ocean, and pups are born between July and December.

LEOPARD SEAL

I'm this big:

This is where I live: icy Antarctic waters

I eat: seabirds, seals, fish, squid, crabs, krill

Bonus fact: As well as eating large animals, I sieve tiny shrimplike krill through my teeth!

Lethal Hunter

The leopard seal is a top predator. It chases its prey underwater and grabs it with strong jaws and sharp teeth. Penguins and other seabirds, smaller seals, fish, and squid are a leopard seal's preferred foods. This seal gets its name from its spotted coat and fierce habits, like those of a real leopard.

Leopard seal

Walrus

Walruses are huge mammals with a thick layer of fatty blubber under their skin that protects them from the cold. Males are bigger than females and often fight each other during the mating season.

Whales and Dolphins

Unlike seals, which are semi-aquatic, whales and dolphins spend all their lives in water. Most live in the ocean, but a few dolphins inhabit rivers. Many grow to a huge size, and the biggest animal in the world is the blue whale. Although they live in water, all whales and dolphins come to the surface to breathe. The name for this mammal group is cetaceans.

Humpback whale

Sieving or Chewing Food

There are two types of whales—baleen whales and toothed whales. Baleen whales, such as the humpback whale, have strips of baleen in their jaws instead of teeth. These act like a sieve. As the whale takes in huge gulps of water, it traps millions of tiny shrimplike krill and small fish to eat. Toothed whales have teeth to chew their food.

Bottlenose dolphin

Like all cetaceans, bottlenose dolphins have smooth, hairless bodies. They can leap high out of the water and breathe air through a blowhole on top of their head. Dolphins hunt prey such as fish, crabs, and squid.

Orca

Also known as killer whales, orcas are in fact a type of dolphin. These huge mammals live in family groups and are clever hunters. They work together to find prey and have even learned to attack sea lions on the shoreline.

HUMPBACK WHALE

I'm this big:

This is where I live: all oceans around the world

I eat: krill, plankton, small fish

Bonus fact: Male humpbacks are known for their "singing." They may do this to attract a mate.

All About Birds

Birds are best known for their ability to fly. They have light but strong skeletons, and most can take to the air on wings. Birds are covered in feathers, and together these feathers make up their plumage. Feathers provide warmth as well as lift for flying. However, not all birds can fly. Baby birds are called chicks, and they hatch from hard-shelled eggs.

Peacock

Red-and-green macaw

Many male birds put on dazzling displays to attract a mate. This peacock has extra-long feathers on its back that can open into a beautiful fan to impress a female.

RED-AND-GREEN MACAW

I'm this big:

This is where I live: forests of northern South America and the drier plains farther south

I eat: nuts, seeds, fruit

Bonus fact: I can live to be more than 50 years old!

Beaks and Bills

Like all birds, this red-and-green macaw is warm-blooded and has a beak, or bill, to eat food with. Bird beaks are different shapes and sizes, depending on what the bird eats. Macaws have strong, curved bills to help them crack nuts.

Blue tit

When chicks hatch, they expect to be fed! Parent birds work hard to find food for their young. This blue tit mother has found a juicy caterpillar for her chicks to eat.

Birds of Prey

Also known as raptors, birds of prey have hooked bills and sharp claws to tear their food apart. Incredible eyesight means that they can spot a meal from far away and then swoop in to grab it. Many birds of prey, such as vultures, eat animals that are already dead. This is called scavenging. At night, owls hunt using their sharp hearing to find mice and voles.

Barn owl

Owls are perfectly suited to hunting in darkness. They fly silently and have keen ears that can pick up tiny movements. This barn owl has a disk-shaped face, which helps to guide sounds toward its ears.

The Egyptian vulture has a long, hooked bill to pick at the bodies of dead animals more easily. Vultures do an important job—they help to keep the environment clean.

Egyptian vulture

Healthy Appetite

From earthworms to rabbits, the common buzzard isn't fussy about what it eats. If it spots a meal from the sky, it will drop rapidly to snatch it up. Buzzards also hunt from trees using their powerful eyesight to spy on small mammals. They are just as at home on the ground, snapping up worms and insects to eat.

Common buzzard

COMMON BUZZARD

I'm this big:

This is where I live: much of Europe and into Asia, in woodland and open fields

I eat: mice, voles, rabbits, other birds, dead animals (carrion), worms, insects

Bonus fact: Male buzzards perform amazing twists and turns in the air to impress a female.

Penguins

These flightless birds are superb swimmers! Their flipper-like wings help them twist and turn in the water, and their feathers are short, thick, and waterproof. All penguins have a layer of fatty blubber to keep them warm. When it's time to have their chicks, penguins gather in big groups called colonies. Most penguins live in chilly habitats in the southern half of the world.

King penguin

Caring for Chicks

Penguins lay one or two eggs that are looked after by both parents. When one goes off to hunt for food, the other parent cares for the eggs. Once hatched, chicks are fed a fishy liquid that their parents produce in their stomachs. Chicks grow quickly but cannot swim until their adult feathers have replaced their fluffy chick down.

The fastest-swimming penguin is the gentoo. It can leap above the waves to escape predators such as orcas. This is called porpoising.

Gentoo penguin

The little penguin really is the littlest penguin! At just over 30 cm (one foot) tall, it might reach your knees. It nests in burrows or caves and is the only penguin to be active at night.

Little penguin

KING PENGUIN

I'm this big:

This is where I live: on islands around northern Antarctica, and southern South America

I eat: fish, krill, squid

Bonus fact: I am the second-biggest member of the penguin family—only emperors are bigger!

Flamingos

These tall, pink-feathered birds live in huge colonies around lakes and lagoons. There may be up to one million birds in a colony. Flamingos wade in the water on long, thin legs, dipping their heads to sweep their bills through the water. There are six types of flamingos, and they all live in warmer parts of the world.

Lesser flamingo

A flamingo's pink feathers are due to what it eats—the pinkness comes from the tiny plants and animals that make up its diet. Lesser flamingos can be pale or dark pink.

Caribbean flamingo

Flamingos lay a single egg in a bowl-shaped nest formed from mud. The gray (grey) fluffy chicks are fed a soupy liquid from their parents' stomachs. It takes two to three years before the chicks' pink feathers grow in.

Filter Feeder

The flamingo's strange-shaped bill curves downward for a reason. This helps the bird to filter tiny plants and animals from the water. To feed, the flamingo opens its bill slightly to allow water in. As it sweeps its head from side to side, bits of food are trapped in tiny hairs on the inside of the bill.

Greater flamingo

GREATER FLAMINGO

I'm this big:

This is where I live: salty lakes, estuaries, and mudflats of Africa, Asia, and southern Europe

I eat: shrimp, tiny plants, worms, and insects that live in the water

Bonus fact: I am the biggest member of the flamingo family.

Ratites

The biggest bird in the world is too heavy to fly. The ostrich has long, powerful legs and can outrun most other animals. With its long neck, small head, and big eyes, this giant bird is good at spotting danger, too. The ostrich belongs to a group of flightless birds called ratites. Other birds in this group include the emu, rhea, cassowary, and kiwi.

Cassowary

The shy cassowary lives in thick forests in Australia. If disturbed by another animal, it uses its sharp-clawed toes to protect itself.

OSTRICH

I'm this big:

This is where I live: : the grasslands of Africa

I eat: roots, seeds, shoots, grass

Bonus fact: I am the only bird with two toes—but beware, my claws are sharp!

On the Move

The ostrich is the fastest bird on two legs. It can run at speeds of 70 km an hour (43 miles an hour) to escape leopards and lions. Males lead small groups of females as they travel long distances every day, looking for grass and seeds to eat.

Ostrich

An ostrich egg is about the size of a melon, and it takes up to 40 days for a chick to hatch.

Kiwi

Kiwis are nocturnal birds, so they look for food at night. They have nostrils at the end of their long bill and use their sharp sense of smell to find worms and insects to eat.

Hummingbirds

These small birds can flap their wings so fast that they make a humming sound. Hummingbirds hover in the air to sip sugary nectar from flowers with their long, thin bills. They can twist and turn quickly in flight and can even fly upside down. There are more than 300 kinds of hummingbirds, and all have bright, shiny feathers.

Sword-billed hummingbird

The sword-billed hummingbird is the only bird in the world to have a bill longer than its body. The long, curved bill reaches deep into flowers so the bird can feed on nectar.

Although adult hummingbirds feed mainly on flower nectar, their chicks are fed a diet of insects. This provides them with the goodness they need to grow.

Broad-billed hummingbird

Smallest of All

The smallest bird in the world, the bee hummingbird lives up to its name—it can sometimes be mistaken for an insect. As it hovers to feed from flowers, its wings beat an incredible 80 times per second. Even its tiny heart beats more than 1,000 times every minute.

Bee hummingbird

BEE HUMMINGBIRD

I'm this big:

This is where I live: on the island of Cuba in the Caribbean Sea

I eat: flower nectar

Bonus fact: I use a lot of energy as I hover and fly, so I must look for food all day long.

Waterbirds

Ducks, geese, and swans belong to a group of birds called waterfowl. They make their homes around rivers, lakes, and waterways where there is a good supply of food. These birds are super swimmers and have strong, webbed feet and waterproof feathers. Most have a layer of body fat to keep them warm in the water.

Greylag goose

To land on water from the air, this greylag goose stretches out its webbed feet and uses its wings like a parachute to slow down.

Mallard ducks

MALLARD DUCK

I'm this big:

This is where I live: ponds, lakes, parks, and rivers throughout Europe and North America

I eat: worms, shrimp, snails, insects, vegetation

Bonus fact: I can turn upside down to feed underwater—this is called dabbling.

42

Swans are large, graceful birds.
Despite its size, the mute swan is
a strong flier. To get airborne from
the water, it flaps its huge wings
and runs across the surface.
Swans usually pair for life.

Keeping Close

Ducklings can swim soon after they've
hatched. Mallard ducklings are covered
in fluffy down that isn't yet waterproof.
Until their adult feathers grow, they
snuggle against their mother for warmth.
The ducklings stay close to their mother
for protection as they swim.

Mute swan

Seabirds

Sea and coastal habitats are packed with food for hungry birds. Seabirds nest on beaches and cliffs in huge numbers. They fly out to sea to catch fish to bring back to their young. Some spend almost their whole lives at sea, flying great distances as they travel back and forth to sunnier, warmer places.

Atlantic puffin

Burrowing Birds

Puffins spend most of their lives at sea and are excellent swimmers. In the spring, puffin beaks turn bright orange, and the puffins come onto land to nest. They dig burrows in the ground with their beaks and feet, and the female lays a single egg. Both parents care for the chick when it hatches, carrying fish in their beaks to the burrow.

Arctic tern

Arctic terns fly thousands of miles from the Arctic north to the Antarctic south. During summer, these cold places have constant daylight. The terns prefer this because it helps them find food.

Northern gannets plunge deep into the sea. They dive headfirst to catch fish, which they grab with long, sharp beaks. Gannets live in huge groups called gannetries.

Northern gannet

ATLANTIC PUFFIN

I'm this big:

This is where I live: on open water and steep cliffs of the North Atlantic Ocean

I eat: sand eels, herring

Bonus fact: A baby puffin is called a puffling.

45

All About Reptiles

The reptile group includes animals such as crocodiles, lizards, snakes, and turtles. All reptiles are cold-blooded. Those that live in cooler parts of the world must warm up their bodies in the sun for them to work properly. If they get too hot, reptiles seek shade or open their mouths to cool down. Reptiles have dry, scaly skin, and almost all lay eggs from which their babies hatch.

Emerald tree boa

This beautifully patterned snake lives in the rain forests of South America. It hides in trees, wrapped around branches, and hunts small mammals or birds.

Baby turtles hatch from eggs their mother has laid in a hole on a beach and then covered with sand. Once hatched, they race to the sea. They spend years feeding and growing in the ocean before females return to land to lay their eggs.

Leatherback turtles

Frilled lizard

If it feels scared or threatened, the frilled lizard of Australia has a clever trick. It raises a flap of skin around its neck to appear bigger—and scarier—to predators. Lizards have developed many ways of keeping safe. Some can even lose a leg or a tail to escape danger, and then grow them back again.

Frilled lizard

FRILLED LIZARD

I'm this big:

This is where I live: forest, woodland, and dry grasslands of northern Australia

I eat: ants and other insects

Bonus fact: If my frilled neck doesn't scare off danger, I stand on my back legs and run!

Crocodiles

Crocodiles and alligators are fierce reptiles that live along rivers, estuaries, and swamps in hot parts of the world. Their powerful jaws are filled with huge teeth that they use to grab prey. All have thick, scaly skin and long, strong tails for swimming. They are deadly predators and will attack any animal that ventures close to the water.

Super Salty

The huge saltwater crocodile lives along river estuaries where the water is salty. It can swim far out to sea and uses its powerful tail to move through the water. This dangerous crocodile can jump out of the water to surprise prey. It is known to live for a long time, perhaps more than 70 years.

Lying just below the surface, this American alligator is hidden from any animal that may come along. Only its eyes and nostrils appear above water, allowing it to see and breathe.

American alligator

The caiman of South America feeds on fish, birds, and crabs. It can also attack bigger animals such as wild pigs and deer. Bony ridges around its eyes make it look as if it's wearing glasses.

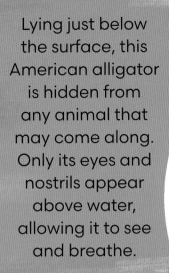

Saltwater crocodile

Spectacled caiman

SALTWATER CROCODILE

I'm this big:

This is where I live: rivers, estuaries, and coastal habitats of northern Australia, eastern India, and Southeast Asia

I eat: almost any animal, from large mammals to fish and birds

Bonus fact: I am the biggest reptile in the world.

Snakes

Even though they don't have legs, snakes move with ease. Their scaly bodies are packed with muscles to push them forward, and they can slither up trees and down into burrows. Snakes have a good sense of smell, and some can detect body heat as they hunt for prey. Some snakes have a venomous bite, while others kill by squeezing, or constriction.

Eastern diamondback rattlesnake

A bony rattle at the tip of a rattlesnake's tail warns attackers away. If the rattle alarm doesn't work, these snakes strike with lightning speed. Their venomous bite can be deadly to humans.

INDIAN PYTHON

I'm this big:

This is where I live: forest, grassland, and swamps of south and Southeast Asia

I eat: mammals, birds, other reptiles

Bonus fact: Baby pythons use an egg tooth to break out of their shells.

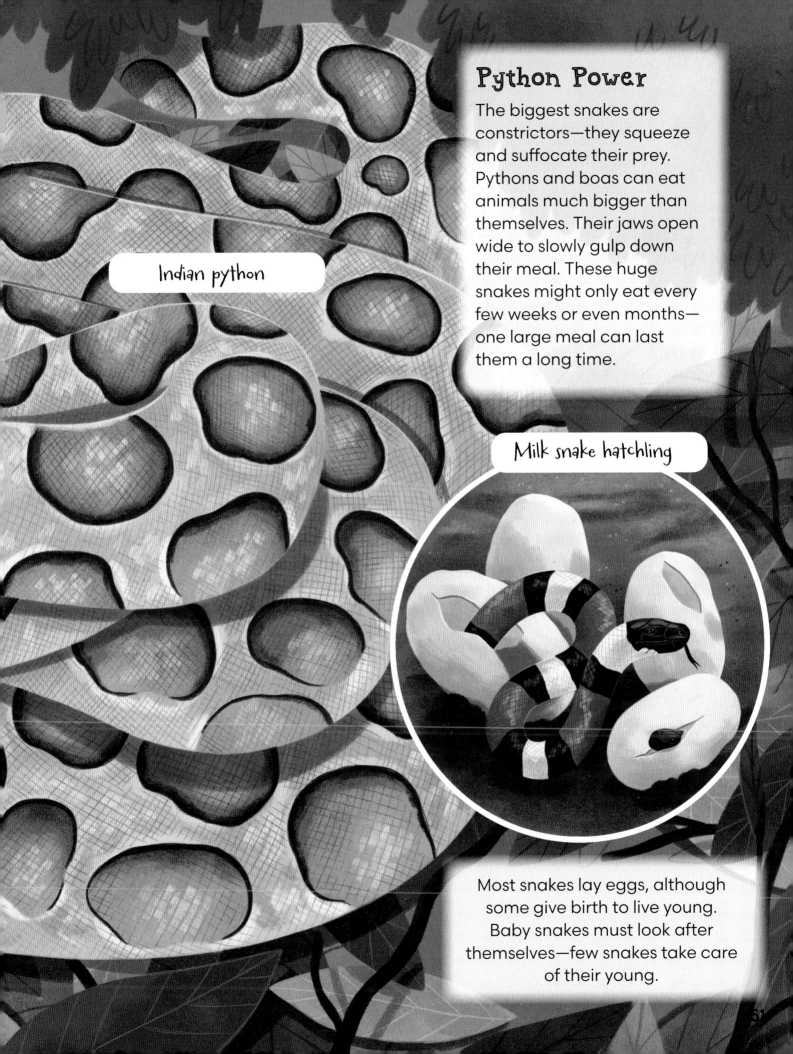

Indian python

Python Power

The biggest snakes are constrictors—they squeeze and suffocate their prey. Pythons and boas can eat animals much bigger than themselves. Their jaws open wide to slowly gulp down their meal. These huge snakes might only eat every few weeks or even months—one large meal can last them a long time.

Milk snake hatchling

Most snakes lay eggs, although some give birth to live young. Baby snakes must look after themselves—few snakes take care of their young.

Tortoises and Turtles

All tortoises and turtles have a hard shell that protects their soft body parts. They live on land as well as in fresh water and the sea, and like most reptiles, they lay eggs from which their young hatch. All have sharp, cutting mouths to eat and catch food, and some types can reach huge sizes.

Alligator snapping turtle

The strong, sharp jaws of this turtle are deadly! It has a piece of skin called a lure in its mouth, which it uses to tempt prey such as frogs and fish. Then, snap! It grabs its prey with great force.

Giant land tortoises live on the Galápagos Islands in the Pacific Ocean. These huge reptiles are not found anywhere else, and they can live more than 100 years.

Galápagos giant tortoise

Green turtle

Sea turtles spend most of their lives in the ocean and come to the surface to breathe. They take long journeys called migrations to return to the beaches where they hatched. Here, they lay their own eggs. Unlike other sea turtles, the green turtle is a herbivore—it eats nothing but plants.

Green turtle

GREEN TURTLE

I'm this big:

This is where I live: oceans and coastal habitats around the world

I eat: sea grasses and plantlike algae

Bonus fact: My diet of green seagrass and tiny plants is what gives me my name—my body fat is green!

Lizards

This large group of reptiles can be found in most habitats across the world. All have dry, scaly skin, four legs, and a tail. Lizards range in size from the tiny nano chameleon, no bigger than a penny, to the huge Komodo dragon. Nearly all lizards lay eggs, and some can give a venomous bite.

Clever Chameleons

With long gripping tails and superlong tongues, chameleons are skilled at catching food in the trees. When they see a tasty insect, they shoot out their sticky tongues at lightning speed to grab it. Chameleons' skin can change from green to red to yellow—and more! These changes depend on if the chameleon is scared, angry, or trying to impress a mate.

Panther chameleon

PANTHER CHAMELEON

I'm this big:

This is where I live: up in the trees on the island of Madagascar in the Pacific Ocean

I eat: insects

Bonus fact: I can swivel my big eyes in different directions.

This gecko has a superpower—its feet are covered in microscopic hairs that help it "stick" to upright surfaces. Tokay geckos have learned to live alongside people—so they might be seen "stuck" to walls!

Tokay gecko

Gila monster

Bright markings on the Gila monster's skin warn other animals to keep away—it's venomous to eat. Its bite is poisonous, too—and it hangs on hard, refusing to let go.

All About Amphibians

Frogs, toads, and salamanders are all amphibians. They walk, crawl, hop, and climb, are cold-blooded, and have smooth or bumpy skin. Most amphibians live on land and near water, and all return to water to breed and lay their eggs. They breathe air and have lungs, and they can also take in air through their skin. Many have poisonous skin, which protects them from predators.

Common spadefoot toad

Toads walk or crawl rather than hop. They have dry, bumpy skin and spend more time on land than frogs. Spadefoot toads use their big feet to dig an underground burrow to live in.

Alpine newt (male)

Newts are a type of salamander. They have a long tail and live both in the water and on land, but they always breed in the water. This male alpine newt has bright markings to attract a mate.

Cycle of Life

A life cycle is how an animal lives from birth or hatching to death, and includes how it has its young. For amphibians, this starts with an egg that hatches into a larva called a tadpole. A tadpole looks very different to the adult it will become. As it feeds and grows, the tadpole changes. A frog tadpole grows legs and loses its tail. Eventually, a tadpole becomes a tiny frog, toad, or salamander. The whole process of change is called metamorphosis.

Common frog

Tadpoles

Frogspawn

COMMON FROG

I'm this big:

This is where I live: ponds, lakes, woodland, yards, and gardens across Europe

I eat: insects, slugs, snails, and worms

Bonus fact: During winter, I hibernate, and bury myself under mud or leaves until spring.

Frogs and Toads

Although frogs and toads look alike, there are a few differences. Frogs have smooth, damp skin and spend more time in water—they have long legs for jumping and swimming. Toads have shorter legs and crawl rather than jump. Both frogs and toads are carnivores and eat bugs, insects, and worms. Some eat bigger animals such as mice and birds.

Midwife toad

Instead of leaving its eggs in water, the male midwife toad carries them on his back! He returns to the water when the tadpoles are ready to hatch.

RED-EYED TREE FROG

I'm this big:

This is where I live: rain forest trees of Central South America

I eat: insects and other small amphibians

Bonus fact: I lay my eggs on a leaf, often near a pool. When my tadpoles hatch they plop into the water or I carry them to water.

Up in the Trees

Special pads on the toes of tree frogs help them to climb up plants and trees. Their green bodies help to hide them among the leaves, but their bright markings may surprise other animals. These little frogs have big, bright-red eyes that may also be useful for staying safe. If predators come too close, the frogs can flash their eyes, and scare the danger away.

Red-eyed tree frog

Natterjack toad

In spring, male natterjack toads gather to "sing" to females. They have a vocal sac in their throat that extends as they croak.

Salamanders

This group of amphibians also includes newts. They have long bodies, short legs, and a tail. Most salamanders live in damp places and return to water to lay their eggs. But their life cycles are not all the same. Some salamanders have lungs to breathe air, while others have no lungs and breathe through their skin.

Fire salamander

Fiery Fiend

The bright skin pattern of the fire salamander is a warning to predators—I am poisonous! The markings can be yellow, red, or orange and the poison can seep and be sprayed from around the salamander's head and back. Fire salamanders live mainly on land, and hunt for food at night. In winter they burrow into the ground to escape the cold.

This strange-looking salamander never grows up! Even as an adult, the axolotl looks like a youngster. It keeps its feathery gills and lives entirely in water.

Axolotl

When spring arrives, male great crested newts "dance" in the water to attract females. After the breeding season, the crest shrinks back into their bodies.

Great crested newt

FIRE SALAMANDER

I'm this big:

I'm this big: This is where I live: cool, damp woodlands in Europe

I eat: worms, slugs, snails, and insects

Bonus fact: my skin is poisonous—so don't touch me!

All About Fish

Fish live entirely in water. They breathe using body parts called gills, and they have fins and a tail to help them swim. Fish are cold-blooded and have a skeleton that is either bony or made of cartilage—a light, flexible material. Most fish lay eggs from which their babies hatch, but some give birth to live young.

Whale shark

The biggest fish in the world is the mighty whale shark. This giant eats tiny food—it opens its huge mouth to filter shrimplike plankton from the water.

SWEETLIPS

I'm this big:

This is where I live: around coral reefs in the Indian Ocean and the Great Barrier Reef in Australia

I eat: starfish, shrimp, shellfish, fish fry, seagrass

Bonus fact: My lips get bigger as I grow older!

Sweetlips

Moray eel

Blending in

These sweetlips fish have bright striped markings that may help them blend in with their coral reef home.

Eels have long bodies and look something like snakes. This moray eel uses its strong sense of smell to find food.

63

Sharks and Rays

Sharks have strong, sleek bodies, and most have deadly jaws packed with teeth. Their skin is covered in toothlike denticles, and they have excellent senses of smell and sight. Rays have flat bodies and big fins that look like wings to help them "fly" through the water. Sharks and rays have a light, flexible skeleton made of cartilage instead of bone.

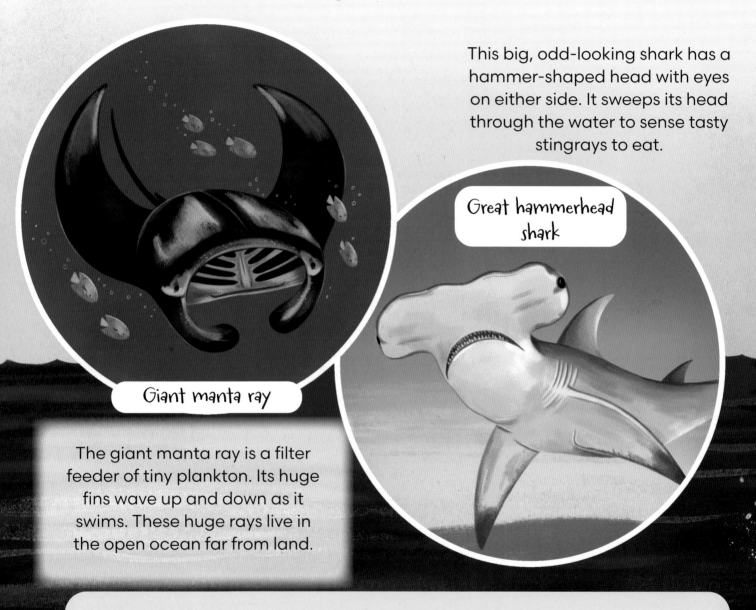

This big, odd-looking shark has a hammer-shaped head with eyes on either side. It sweeps its head through the water to sense tasty stingrays to eat.

Great hammerhead shark

Giant manta ray

The giant manta ray is a filter feeder of tiny plankton. Its huge fins wave up and down as it swims. These huge rays live in the open ocean far from land.

GREAT WHITE SHARK

I'm this big:

This is where I live: worldwide in warmer oceans, open and coastal waters

I eat: seals, sea lions, whales, seabirds, big fish

Bonus fact: My sharp teeth are constantly replaced by new ones—so I never lose my bite.

Perfect Predator

The great white shark is a fierce and clever hunter. It has a huge, powerful body and jaws filled with supersharp teeth. Great whites can warm their blood to keep their muscles working hard. Then they attack prey rapidly.

Great white shark

Leafy Sea Dragon

Some fish really don't look like fish at all! The leafy sea dragon belongs to the same family that includes seahorses and pipefish. Its body is covered in floaty, leaflike strands that make it look like a floating clump of seaweed. Leafy sea dragons swim slowly using tiny fins. They suck up food from the water with their long snout.

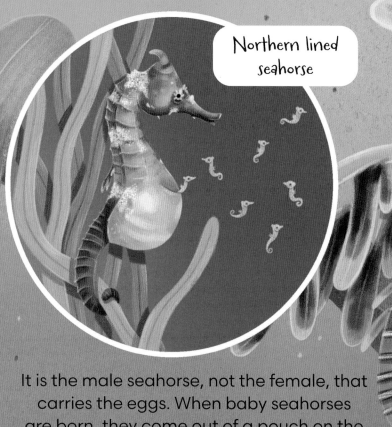

Northern lined seahorse

It is the male seahorse, not the female, that carries the eggs. When baby seahorses are born, they come out of a pouch on the male's stomach. The tiny babies float in the ocean where they grow bigger.

LEAFY SEA DRAGON

I'm this big:

This is where I live: calm, shallow waters around southern Australia

I eat: tiny shrimp, lice

Bonus fact: Sea dragons don't have scales—they have bony plates to protect their bodies.

Clever Camouflage

Many animals use camouflage to help them blend in with their surroundings, and the leafy sea dragon is an expert. The long, leafy strands on its body help to hide it from other fish that might snap it up. Sea dragons are poor swimmers, so they can't escape bigger fish. Blending in and staying hidden are the best ways for them to stay safe.

Banded pipefish

Leafy sea dragon

Pipefish have long, thin bodies. This male pipefish is carrying lots of eggs on his stomach, from which baby pipefish will hatch.

Reef Fish

Coral reefs are home to fish of all shapes, sizes, and patterns. Here, the water is warm and clear, and there is lots of food. Reef fish often have bright markings and clever ways of keeping safe from predators. The parrotfish nibbles its food from rocky coral. Any coral that it eats is broken down in its stomach—and comes out the other end as sand.

The lionfish is covered in bright stripes to warn other animals away. If that doesn't work, the long, thin spines on its back serve as a venomous weapon.

Lionfish

Some fish have learned clever ways to stay safe. Clownfish live among the stinging arms of sea anemones. The clownfish are covered in slime that protects them from the stings.

Clownfish

Ocean Parrot

The beaky mouth of the parrotfish is made up of two rows of sharp teeth that are joined together. The parrotfish eats algae, which are tiny plants that live on the coral. As the fish nibbles and scrapes the coral, it eats algae there.

Parrotfish

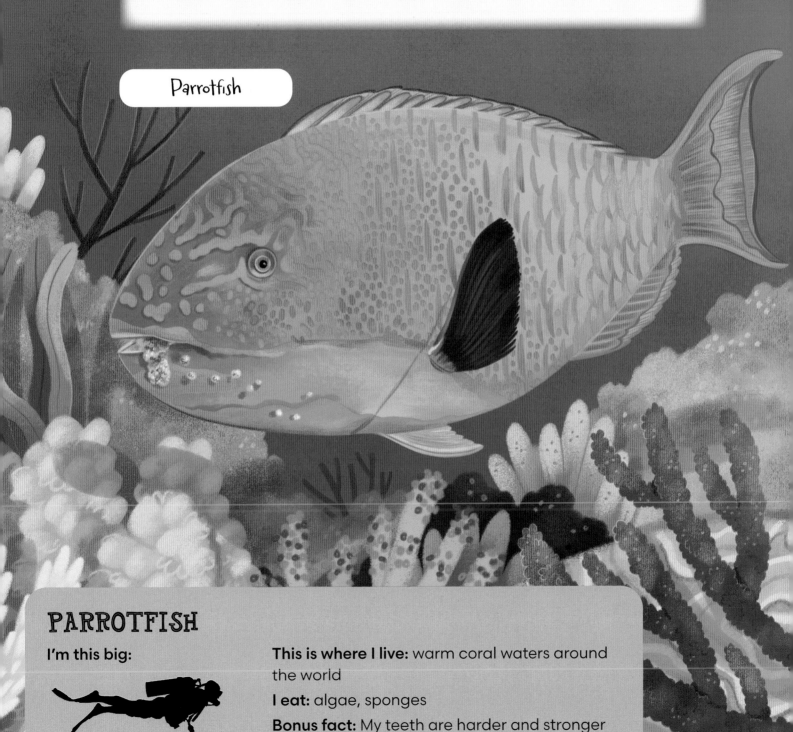

PARROTFISH

I'm this big:

This is where I live: warm coral waters around the world

I eat: algae, sponges

Bonus fact: My teeth are harder and stronger than some metals.

Open Ocean Fish

The open ocean is home to some of the biggest and fastest-swimming fish. Here, shoals of smaller fish are food for hunters such as the sailfish. This predator can swim at more than 50 km an hour (30 miles an hour), making it one of the speediest fish in the ocean. Its body is packed with powerful muscles to help it twist and turn in the water.

Atlantic sailfish

ATLANTIC SAILFISH

I'm this big:

This is where I live: warmer open waters of the Atlantic Ocean

I eat: sardines, mackerel, anchovies, tuna, octopus, squid

Bonus fact: The "sail" on my back can be taller than the length of my body!

Tuna are fast, fierce ocean hunters. These giant fish use their sharp eyesight to track down smaller fish to eat.

With its huge, round body and beaky mouth, the sunfish is an odd-looking creature. It is the biggest fish with a bony skeleton and can grow to be bigger than a person is tall.

Built for Speed

Sailfish have a long, strong body and a tall, sail-like fin stretching along their back. These speedy fish hunt in packs to round up shoals of smaller fish, making them bunch up into a huge fishy ball. Then it's easy for the sailfish to dart in and pick off what they want to eat with their long, pointed jaws.

Ocean sunfish

71

Deep Sea Fish

The deep ocean is home to some of the strangest fish. In this habitat, the water is very cold, and there is no light. Anglerfish have a clever way of attracting food. They have what looks like their very own fishing rod and light! This is a spiny piece of a fin, and it dangles above the head to tempt other fish to it. Then the anglerfish snaps them up.

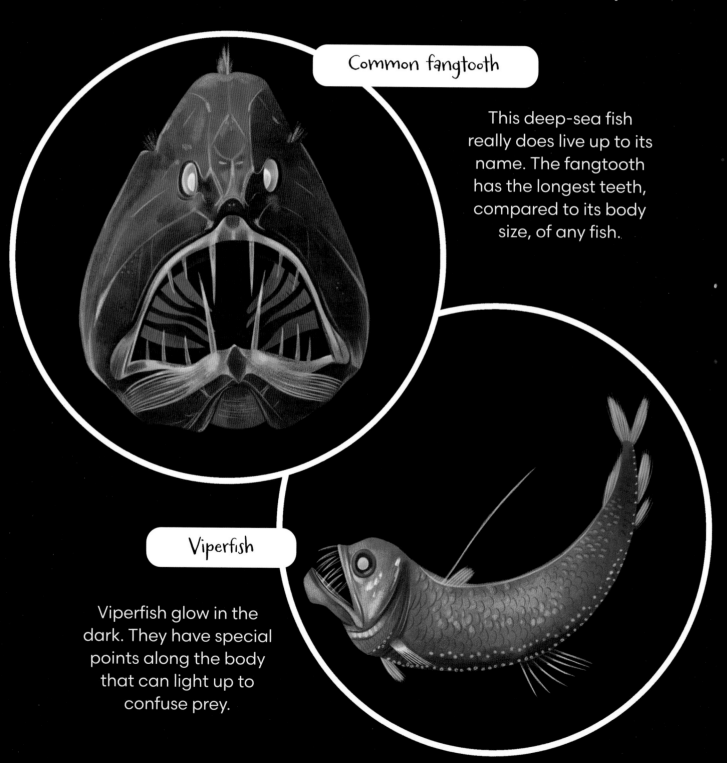

Common fangtooth

This deep-sea fish really does live up to its name. The fangtooth has the longest teeth, compared to its body size, of any fish.

Viperfish

Viperfish glow in the dark. They have special points along the body that can light up to confuse prey.

Monster of the Deep

On an anglerfish's head is a long growth, shaped like a fishing rod. At its end is a "lure" which dangles over the anglerfish's mouth. Like many creatures of the deep, the anglerfish has the ability to produce its own light. It lights up the lure to attract prey, which it sucks into its large mouth.

Humpback anglerfish

HUMPBACK ANGLERFISH

I'm this big:

This is where I live: very deep water in warmer oceans

I eat: fish, squid, shrimp, eels, dead animals

Bonus fact: The tiny male lives permanently attached to the female and is fed by her blood supply.

All About Invertebrates

An invertebrate is an animal without a backbone. Insects, spiders, slugs, worms, and jellyfish are all types of invertebrates. There are more invertebrate animals living on Earth than all the other animal groups put together. Many invertebrates, such as worms in the soil, help to keep the environment clean by feeding on rotting plants and animal poop.

Giant desert centipede

This giant desert centipede has more than 40 legs! Centipedes kill their prey by biting it and injecting venom. They eat insects, frogs, and lizards.

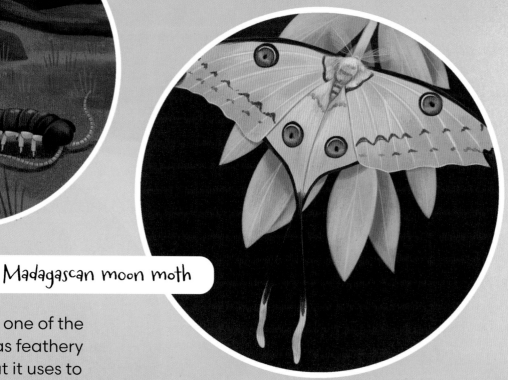

Madagascan moon moth

The beautiful moon moth is one of the biggest kinds of moths. It has feathery feelers called antennae that it uses to sense the world around it.

BLUEBOTTLE AND GREENBOTTLE FLY

I'm this big:

This is where I live: worldwide, in all warmer habitats

I eat: dead or rotting animals, pollen, nectar

Bonus fact: I lay my eggs in animal poop so they can hatch into maggots.

Bluebottle

Food from Flies

Flies are helpful recyclers of rotting things. Lots of other animals eat flies, too. Flies belong to the insect family. They have wings, a body made up of three parts, and six legs. Bluebottles and greenbottles are blowflies. Their bodies are bright and shiny. They have huge eyes and a good sense of smell.

Bees and Wasps

Bees and wasps are insects. Like most insects, they can fly, and some kinds make nests and live in big groups. Wasps have bright markings that warn other animals they can sting. Flowering plants rely on these insects to spread dusty pollen so that new plants can grow. Bees have an excellent sense of smell. This helps them find the best flowers to visit for a sweet-tasting liquid called nectar.

Common wasp

Wasps make a nest by chewing bits of wood to make sticky, papery glue. Worker wasps hunt for insects and bring them back to the nest to feed the young.

HONEYBEE

I'm this big:

This is where I live: worldwide in warmer places

I eat: nectar, pollen, honey

Bonus fact: If I find a good source of food, I "dance" to tell the other bees where to find it.

Busy Bees

Honeybees live together in a nest where they care for the queen bee and the young. Bees work together to visit flowers and gather nectar and pollen. They feed this to their young, called larvae. Inside the nest, the eggs grow in special cells made by the bees. The honey made by bees is also good for other animals—and people—to eat. Honeybees are useful insects because they help new plants to grow.

Honeybee

Buff-tailed bumblebee

These bumblebees are covered in fluffy hairs. When a bee visits flowers to gather food, the pollen sticks to the hairs. It then rubs off onto new flowers that the bee visits, helping more plants to grow.

Ants

Ants live in huge numbers, forming a colony that lives in a nest. These busy insects work together to keep the nest clean and safe, find food, and look after the queen and the young. These insects are strong for their size and can carry food in their jaws that is many times heavier than they are.

Leafcutter ant

Leafcutter ants carry big leaves back to their nest. The leaves are used to grow a fungus that the ants like to eat.

Ants can give a nasty nip! Bulldog ants are found in Australia. They have huge jaws that they use to attack other ants and insects.

Bulldog ant

BLACK GARDEN ANT

I'm this big:

This is where I live: worldwide in an underground nest, in yards, gardens, woodlands, parks, forests

I eat: honeydew, pollen, other insects, fruit

Bonus fact: In summer, worker ants grow wings and fly out of the nest in huge numbers.

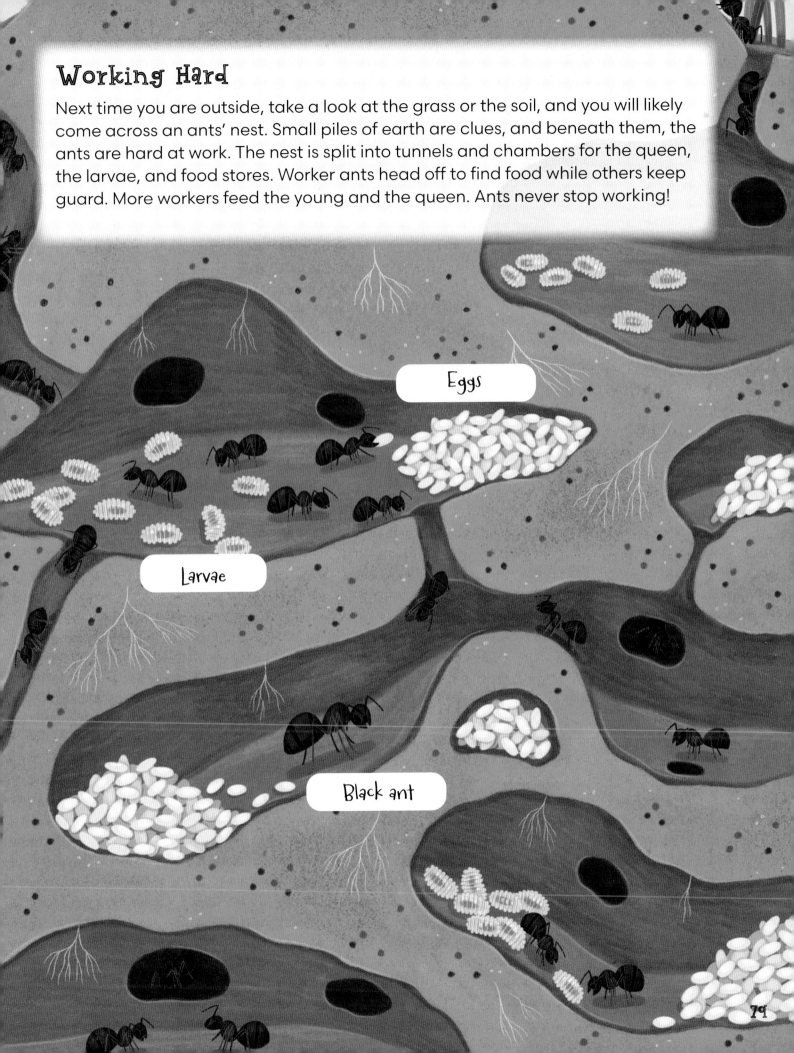

Working Hard

Next time you are outside, take a look at the grass or the soil, and you will likely come across an ants' nest. Small piles of earth are clues, and beneath them, the ants are hard at work. The nest is split into tunnels and chambers for the queen, the larvae, and food stores. Worker ants head off to find food while others keep guard. More workers feed the young and the queen. Ants never stop working!

Eggs

Larvae

Black ant

Beetles

There are many kinds of beetles. Many have wings that are protected by a hard outer casing that opens for flight. Most beetles lay eggs from which their young hatch. The young are called larvae, and they eat as much as possible before changing into a pupa, and finally, an adult beetle.

Hercules beetle

Rhinoceros beetles, like this Hercules beetle, have hornlike growths on their head. These beetles are very strong for their size, and fighting males can lift each other off the ground.

Firefly

Flashing fireflies are beetles that light up the night. Special chemicals in the fireflies' bodies help them glow and flash messages to each other.

Wonderful Wings

Beetles are often beautiful. Their hard, shiny wing cases can be red, green, blue, spotted, or striped. The seven-spotted ladybird (or ladybug) has brilliant red wing cases with black spots. These are called elytra. To fly, the beetle opens its wing cases and spreads its flying wings. After it lands, the elytra close to protect the delicate flight wings.

Ladybug
(Ladybird)

LADYBUG OR LADYBIRD

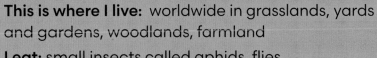

I'm this big:

This is where I live: worldwide in grasslands, yards and gardens, woodlands, farmland

I eat: small insects called aphids, flies

Bonus fact: My bright-red wing cases warn other animals not to eat me—I taste awful.

Butterflies and Moths

Fluttering butterflies and moths are some of the most beautiful of all insects. They have two pairs of wings that can have incredible markings and patterns. Butterflies are most often seen in summer, flying from flower to flower to feed on sugary nectar. Most moths fly in the evening. These insects go through a special change before they can fly as adults.

Monarch butterfly

Larvae

Eggs

Pupa

Butterfly emerging from pupa

Life Cycle

First, an adult butterfly lays its eggs on plants. When the eggs hatch, the young are known as larvae—we call them caterpillars. During this stage, a caterpillar munches its way through as many plants as it can. The caterpillar then forms a pupa, where it is safely wrapped up to begin its change into a butterfly. Finally, the adult butterfly breaks out of the pupa, spreads its wings, and flies away!

Monarch butterflies fly up to 4,000 km (2,500 miles) to lay their eggs in warmer places. Then they rest over the winter.

Monarch butterfly

Elephant hawk moth

Hawk moths are speedy fliers and beat their wings quickly using strong muscles. This hawk moth is flying at night, searching for sugary flower nectar to drink.

MONARCH BUTTERFLY

I'm this big:

This is where I live: mainly Canada and the USA in farmland, parks, yards, and gardens, wherever milkweed grows

I eat: sugary flower nectar

Bonus fact: I will only lay my eggs on milkweed, which is what my caterpillars like to eat.

83

Dragonflies

If you see a flash of sparkling blue on a summer's day, it could be a dragonfly. These insects are fast fliers. They dart about near rivers and lakes, and their shiny wings and long bodies catch the light. Dragonflies are fierce hunting insects. They have huge eyes and strong jaws, and some can catch prey as they fly.

Beautiful demoiselle damselfly

Damselflies are smaller than dragonflies, with longer, thinner bodies. This damselfly has two pairs of wide, blue wings.

Dragonflies lay their eggs in the water. When baby dragonflies hatch, they are called larvae or nymphs. They live in water hunting tadpoles, snails, and worms until they change into an adult.

Emperor dragonfly nymph

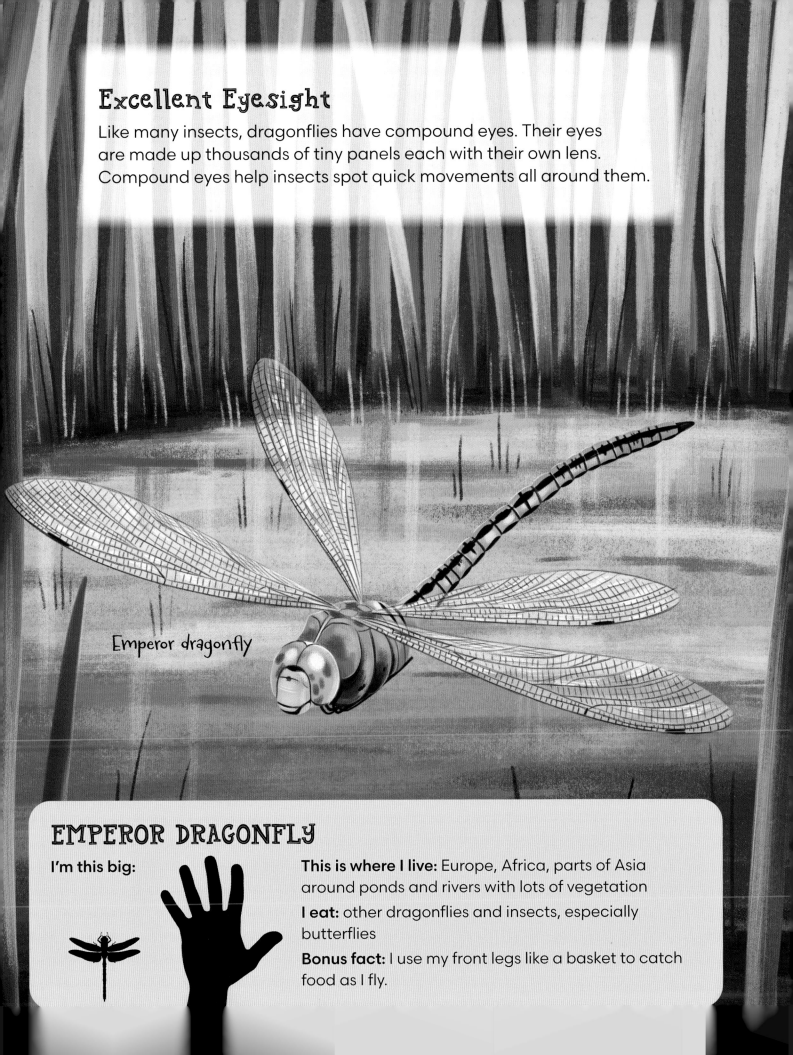

Excellent Eyesight

Like many insects, dragonflies have compound eyes. Their eyes are made up thousands of tiny panels each with their own lens. Compound eyes help insects spot quick movements all around them.

Emperor dragonfly

EMPEROR DRAGONFLY

I'm this big:

This is where I live: Europe, Africa, parts of Asia around ponds and rivers with lots of vegetation

I eat: other dragonflies and insects, especially butterflies

Bonus fact: I use my front legs like a basket to catch food as I fly.

Spiders

With eight legs and many eyes, not everyone likes spiders. But without them, insects such as flies would be everywhere. Spiders play a very important role in nature. They are carnivores, which means that they eat other animals. Spiders produce silk, a special material they use to build their webs. Sticky webs are used to catch prey. Some spiders can give a nasty bite, but most are harmless to people.

Wonderful Webs

Spiderwebs are incredible. They are built with silk that the spider makes in its body in an organ called a spinneret. This web belongs to a garden spider. The spider can build a new web every night to trap insects to eat. Silk is a very strong, sticky material that holds prey fast. The spider then bites its prey and wraps it up in more silk to eat later.

GARDEN SPIDER

I'm this big:

This is where I live: yards, gardens, woodlands, meadows, forests across Europe, the Middle East, and North America

I eat: insects such as flies, butterflies, and moths

Bonus fact: My babies are called spiderlings.

Tarantula

Some spiders are huge! Tarantulas live in warmer parts of the world. They don't build webs but use their silk to line their burrows. They have big fangs to bite prey with.

Crab spider

This crab spider can change its body to match its background. It sits and waits for prey to land, and then it pounces and bites.

Slugs and Snails

Some invertebrates move on one foot! Slugs and snails of different types live on land and in water. They have soft, slimy bodies that move on a muscular "foot." To sense the world around them they have tentacles—long, thin body parts with eyes, on top of their heads. Snails have a spiral shell that protects their soft body, but slugs do not. These creatures like damp, cool places to live. Many kinds live in rivers and oceans too.

Garden snail

GARDEN SNAIL

I'm this big:

This is where I live: woodlands, yards, gardens, hedgerows, fields, grasslands of Europe

I eat: plants and flowers, and sometimes dead worms!

Bonus fact: I have lots of tiny teeth that help me eat my food.

The nudibranch is also called a sea slug. Many have beautiful patterns, and they crawl slowly over the seabed looking for food such as sponges and sea anemones. Sea slugs have a set of feathery gills to take oxygen from the water.

Sea slug (nudibranch)

With no shell to protect them, slugs are most active at night, especially after rain. Their thick, slimy bodies help them slide slowly along as they feed on leaves and plants.

Leopard slug

Slow as a Snail

Slimy snails move slowly on their muscly "foot." They leave a trail of slime as they crawl along, munching plants. A snail's eyes are at the tip of its tentacles, and near its mouth is a set of feelers that it uses to find food. Snails are a good source of food for other animals, especially birds.

Octopuses and Squid

Octopuses and squid live in the ocean. All octopuses have eight flexible arms covered in rows of suckers, and a beaky mouth for eating prey. Squid have eight arms, plus two extra near their mouth that they use to eat their prey. Octopuses live alone, but some types of squid may form groups called shoals.

Bigfin reef squid

At night, bigfin reef squid rise up from deep water to feed. They live in shoals and are iridescent, so their skin shimmers in reflective light.

With wavy tentacles, the nautilus belongs to the same animal group as octopuses and squid. Its body is protected by a hard shell.

Chambered nautilus

Clever Octopus

The giant Pacific octopus hunts along the seabed for crunchy crabs. With its eight curling arms, it can scoot quickly through the water to grab food. If it is scared, it quickly changes its skin to blend in with its surroundings. It can also squirt jets of black ink into the water to confuse predators. Its body is so soft and squishy, it can squeeze into tiny rocky spaces to hide.

Giant Pacific octopus

GIANT PACIFIC OCTOPUS

I'm this big:

This is where I live: shallower water along the seabed and coral reefs in the northern Pacific Ocean

I eat: shellfish, crabs, fish

Bonus fact: I have three hearts, and my blood is blue!

Jellyfish

With long, trailing tentacles and soft, bell-shaped bodies, jellyfish drift or swim through the ocean. These strange invertebrates aren't fish at all. They are very simple creatures without skeletons or body parts such as hearts or brains. In fact, they are mainly made up of water. Most jellyfish eat other animals, and their tentacles are covered in stings that they use to kill their prey.

Lion's mane jellyfish

LION'S MANE JELLYFISH

I'm this big:

This is where I live: colder, open waters of the Arctic, Atlantic, and Pacific Oceans

I eat: fish, shellfish, and other jellyfish

Bonus fact: I am the biggest kind of jellyfish, and I can glow in the dark.

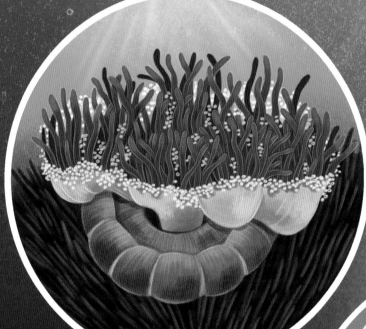

Upside-down jellyfish

Some jellyfish have algae living in their tentacles. The algae need light to survive, so the jellyfish turns upside down to let light from the surface reach its tentacles. The algae make sugars that feed the jellyfish.

Papuan jellyfish

Floating Stings

With its long, thin tentacles, the lion's mane jellyfish really does look like a floating lion's mane. If fish or other animals touch the stings, they are stunned, which means that they can't move. The jellyfish pulls the prey into its mouth inside its body. These jellyfish can grow to huge sizes and have more than 1,000 stinging tentacles.

To move, jellyfish use their muscles to squeeze their bell-shaped body. Water is forced out of the body, which pushes the jellyfish along.

Glossary

algae
Simple organisms that grow mainly in water. Algae are food for animals such as fish.

amphibian
An animal such as a frog, a toad, or a newt. Amphibians are cold-blooded and lay their eggs in water.

baleen
Strips of flexible material in the mouths of some whales. Baleen helps the whales to filter food from the water.

bill
The beak of a bird.

blubber
A thick layer of fat that sea animals have. Blubber helps animals such as penguins and seals keep warm.

camouflage
How an animal's fur or skin blends in with grass, trees, water, or other natural backgrounds. This makes the animal difficult to see and hides it from hunters.

canine
Dogs, wolves, and foxes are types of canines. They have long jaws, can run fast, and have a good sense of smell.

carnivore
An animal that eats other animals.

cartilage
A light, strong material that some animals have instead of a bony skeleton. Sharks and rays have a skeleton made of cartilage.

caterpillar
The young of butterflies and moths. Caterpillars hatch from eggs.

cetacean
Whales and dolphins are cetaceans. They are mammals that live in the ocean and come to the surface to breathe air.

cold-blooded
Describes an animal that has no internal mechanism to control its own body temperature.

colony (colonies)
A group of animals that live together in huge numbers. Some kinds of birds, insects, and mammals live in colonies.

communicate
The way animals share information. Wolves communicate with each other by howling, growling, and moving their bodies in a certain way.

constrictor
A type of snake that kills its prey by squeezing it. Pythons are constrictors.

denticles
Rough scales on the skin of sharks.

echolocation
The way that some animals find their way in the dark and hunt for food. Bats squeak to make sound waves that bounce off insects. The sound returns to the bat like an echo. This tells the bat where the insect is.

elytra
Hard wing cases that cover the wings of beetles.

energy
Animals need energy to live and move their bodies. Energy comes from the food that animals eat.

environment
The natural world, such as the surroundings where animals live on land and in water.

estuary (estuaries)
Where a river meets the sea. Crocodiles live in estuaries.

filter feeder
Animals with special parts in their mouths or their beaks. These parts trap tiny plants and animals in water. Some sharks, whales, and birds are filter feeders.

fish
Cold-blooded animals that live and breathe in water, such as sharks.

flippers
Body parts that help some sea creatures swim, such as penguins, dolphins, and seals.

fungus/fungi
A living thing that grows in the soil or on rotting plants. Some animals, such as ants, eat fungi.

gills
Body parts on fish and some kinds of amphibians. Gills help these animals to breathe in water.

grassland
A large area of land in which lots of different types of grasses grow. Many animals live in grasslands, such as lions and zebra.

habitat
The place where an animal lives. A habitat can be in water, in a forest, or in a desert. Polar bears live in a cold polar habitat.

herbivore
An animal that feeds only on plants, such as rabbits and hares.

hibernate/hibernation
During winter, there is less food for some animals. They find a safe place to sleep to keep warm. They hibernate until spring.

insect
Animals with six legs, three main body sections, and wings. Most insects can fly.

invertebrate
An animal without a backbone, such as an octopus.

krill
Tiny living things in the ocean, such as baby shrimp and crabs. Many animals eat krill, such as penguins, fish, and whales.

larva (larvae)
The young form of organisms that changes form during their lives. Caterpillars are the larvae of butterflies.

life cycle
The stages in an animal's life, from when it is born until it dies.

maggot
The young, or larvae, of flies that look like tiny worms. Maggots hatch from eggs.

mammal
A warm-blooded animal that has a backbone, gives birth to live young, and feeds them on milk.

marsupial
A mammal that gives birth to tiny babies that live and grow in a pouch. Kangaroos are marsupials.

meadow
An area of land in which grasses and wildflowers grow. Lots of animals live in meadows, such as birds and insects.

metamorphosis
A life stage where animals such as insects and amphibians go through changes to become adults.

migration (migrate)
A long journey that some animals make. They do this to spend time in warmer places to have their young and find food. Lots of birds, mammals, and insects migrate.

nectar
The sweet liquid that plants make. Insects such as bees feed on nectar.

nocturnal
If an animal is more active at night than during the day, it is nocturnal. Bats are nocturnal.

nudibranch
A type of mollusk (mollusc) that lives in the sea and breathes using gills.

omnivore
An animal that eats plants and other animals.

oxygen
The gas that all living things need to survive. Mammals breathe in oxygen from the air. Fish use gills to breathe oxygen in water.

pinniped
Seals, sea lions, and walruses are pinnipeds. They are mammals with flippers that live in the ocean and on land.

plains
Large, flat areas of land that can be hot, cold, wet, or dry. Many animals live on plains.

plankton
Tiny plants and animals that float in the ocean. Plankton is food for animals such as fish.

plumage
The covering of feathers on a bird's body.

pollen
A powdery substance made by plants that helps them reproduce. Many insects, such as bees, spread pollen.

predator
An animal that hunts and eats other animals. Tigers are predators.

prey
An animal that is hunted for food by another animal. Deer are prey for tigers.

pupa (pupae)
The stage in an insect's life before it is an adult. A pupa is covered by a hard casing, and inside the insect's body changes. Caterpillars turn into pupae, then into butterflies.

rain forest
A huge area of land in which lots of trees and plants grow. Rain forests are wet and warm. They are home to lots of animals.

raptor
A bird with a sharp bill and claws that hunts other animals. Buzzards are raptors.

reproduce
An animal having its young. Amphibians lay eggs, and mammals give birth. All animals reproduce.

reptile
A cold-blooded animal with scaly skin. Most reptiles lay eggs. Lizards and snakes are reptiles.

scavenger
An animal that eats dead animals. Vultures are scavengers.

senses
All animals have senses such as sight, hearing, smell, and touch. Senses tell animals about the world around them.

silk
A strong, stretchy material that spiders make in their bodies. Spiders use silk to build their webs or line their burrows.

skeleton
The hard, bony framework that supports an animal's body. Cats have a strong skeleton that helps them leap and run. Sharks have a skeleton made of cartilage.

sound wave
When sounds travel through the air, they create vibrations known as sound waves. Bats use these to find food and get around.

species
One particular kind of living thing. Members of the same species often look similar and produce fertile offspring together.

swamp
A large, wet area of land with rivers or lakes. Alligators live in swamps.

tentacle
A long, flexible organ used to sense, grab, or move around on. A squid has tentacles.

tropical
Hot, wet conditions or places. Most rain forests are tropical.

tundra
Cold northern areas of land with frozen soil and no trees. Some plants grow here. Animals such as Arctic hares live on the tundra.

venomous
Describes an animal that can give a sting or a bite that releases a harmful substance called venom.

vertebrate
An animal with a backbone, such as a mammal or bird.

warm-blooded
Mammals are warm-blooded. Their body temperature stays the same whatever the temperature of their surroundings.

waterfowl
Birds such as swans, geese, and ducks that live by rivers, lakes, and estuaries.

waterproof
If something is waterproof, it keeps water out. Penguins have waterproof feathers to keep them warm and dry in water.

Index

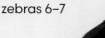